The Native Americans Who Changed the World Biography Kids

Children's United States Biographies

BABY PROFESSOR

EDUCATION KIDS

In this book, let's walk the trail of some great Native Americans, and find out how they made their mark on the world.

The first people

Long before Europeans "discovered the New World" of North and South America, the two continents were full of people of many different cultures. The first people in North America arrived from Asia about 30,000 years ago, walking across a land bridge that existed at that time between Siberia and Alaska.

People spread into every part of North and South America, creating great empires in some areas and living in small-scale balance with the land in others. There were more than 250 different Native American languages spoken in what is now the United States.

All that changed when the Europeans arrived. They brought superior technology, like guns; but beyond that they brought diseases against which the Native Americans had no defences. Millions of people died from measles and smallpox, and whole indigenous cultures disappeared.

Since the arrival of Europeans, Native Americans have fought a defensive war to try to preserve their land and way of life. White Americans have sometimes treated Native Americans harshly, using violence and breaking solemn treaties to clear the way for further expansion.

Great Native Americans

All through their history, Native Americans have had great heroes. Here are some that we know of because they lived and acted at a time when people wrote down what they did.

Squanto (1581-1622)

Squanto, a Patuxet living in what is now Massachusetts, was captured along with others in 1608 by English traders. The traders took the Native Americans to England as if they were zoo animals. In England Squanto learned English, and his descriptions of his homeland helped inspire the plan to found a colony. When Squanto finally returned to his home after five years, he found that everyone in his tribe had died of the plague, a disease brought by fleas on the rats in European ships.

Squanto was central in helping make peace and promote understanding between the tribes and the new colony of Pilgrims at Plymouth, Massachusetts in 1620. He helped the colony survive through a harsh winter.

Pontiac (1720-1769)

Chief Pontiac led the Ottawa tribe in battle against the British, attempting to keep them from occupying tribal territory around the Great Lakes, in what is now known as Chief Pontiac's War. He attacked Fort Detroit and finally captured it after The Battle of Bloody Run. Pontiac was a great leader, but later came into conflict with his tribe and went to the ancient city Cahokia in what is now Illinois. There a member of the Peoria tribe killed him.

Black Hawk (1767-1838)

Black Hawk was a war captain, not a chief. In the War of 1812, he led the Sauk tribe in support of the British. He died much later during a raid on settlers in Iowa. Many Native Americans consider him a resistance hero.

Sequoiah (1767-1843)

Sequoiah, a Cherokee, was also known as George Guest. He worked as a silversmith and invented the writing system for his tribe: the Cherokee Syllabry.

Tecumseh (1768-1813)

Tecumseh was a Shawnee military and spiritual leader. He was involved in a religious awakening in which the prophet Tenskwatawa called on the people to reject English ways and stop giving away their land. Not all leaders agreed with Tecumseh and Tenskwatawa, and they eventually moved northwest into what is now Indiana. There they founded Prophetstown. Tecumseh died during the War of 1812.

Sacajawea (1788-1812)

Sacajawea has a place in the American story for her role as a guide to the Lewis and Clark Expedition to the Pacific Ocean in 1805-6. She was known as "Salmon Eater", or "Agaidika", in her Shoshone tribe. She famously gave birth to a son while on the trail, and then continued the journey. Sacajawea's image appears on the U.S. one-dollar coin.

Red Cloud (1822-1909)

Red Cloud, or "Makhpiya Luta" in Sioux, was a great leader of his people in both war and peace. He fought the U.S. Army in Wyoming and Montana during "Red Cloud's War", and continued to lead the tribe when the war was over and they were settled on a reservation.

Cochise (1815-1874)

Apache warrior Cochise fought both the Mexicans and the Americans to resist settlement in traditional Apache land.

Geronimo (1829-1909)

Geronimo, "He Who Yawns", led the Chricahua Apache in a defensive struggle against both Mexico and the expanding United States for more than 20 years. He was both a military and spiritual leader, though not a chief. He was at the head of the last great uprising by Native Americans.

Sitting Bull (1831-1890)

Sitting Bull was a Lakota medicine man and spiritual leader. He had a vision that the Sioux would win a great victory in the Black Hills of Montana. Thousands of Sioux and Cheyenne warriors destroyed a U.S. Cavalry force led by General George Armstrong Custer at what Native Americans call The Battle of the Greasy Grass, or in English The Battle of Little Big Horn. For Native Americans, Sitting Bull's spiritual and cultural contributions to his people are as important as the battle.

Will Rogers (1879-1935)

Will Rogers, of Cherokee descent, was a hugely-popular entertainer and public speaker. He performed on stage and in rodeos and Wild-West shows, with an act that ranged from story-telling and comedy to showing off his skills with a lasso and as a horse rider. The Guinness Book of World Records listed Will for using three lassos at the same time to snare a horse and rider—one lasso went around the horse's neck, another around all four legs, and the third around the rider.

He toured the world several times and appeared in 71 movies, both silent films and "talkies". He was sometimes called "Oklahoma's Favorite Son". He wrote over 4,000 columns that appeared in newspapers across the country, combining humor and sly commentary on public affairs. "I don't tell jokes," he wrote. "I just watch the government and report the facts."

Jim Thorpe (1887-1953)

Jim Thorpe, or "Bright Path", was a Native American from Oklahoma. As a child, he developed strength and endurance by learning traditional methods of hunting and trapping. At Carlisle Indian Industrial School in Pennsylvania, in 1907, he became a star on the track team.

He was a standout at hockey, lacrosse, baseball and even ballroom dancing, but he became famous as a football player. In the 1912 Olympics in Sweden, Jim won gold medals for the pentathlon and decathlon. The King of Sweden called Jim the greatest athlete in the whole world.

Jim went on to professional sports careers in football and baseball. After retiring as an athlete, he appeared in over 60 Hollywood movies. He used his position to encourage movie-makers to hire more Native Americans as actors.

Maria Tallchief (1925-2013)

Elizabeth Marie Tall Chief, a member of the Osage Nation, started studying ballet when she was three years old. She became a talented ballerina, appearing in many roles. When George Balanchine founded the New York City Ballet in 1947, Maria became the company's star, or prima ballerina.

She was the first Native American to hold such a title. She became world-famous for her skill and innovations, and danced with ballet companies around the world. Later she founded the ballet school of the Chicago Lyric Opera and directed the Chicago City Ballet.

The Code Talkers

The Code Talkers were Native Americans who served in the U.S. military during World War I and World War II. They used codes based on indigenous languages to pass critical information. Spies or those overhearing a radio transmission could not break the codes.

MARINE
CODE
TALKER

The most famous group of Code Talkers were over 400 Navajo soldiers who worked in communications with the U.S. Marines during World War II. The bilingual Code Talkers baffled Japanese forces in the war in the Pacific and kept military communications secure. Chester Nez, the last of the original group of Navajo Code Talkers, died in 2016.

Fritz Scholder (1937-2005)

Fritz Scholder, whose grandmother was a member of the Luiseño tribe, was a painter fascinated with color. He depicted traditional Native American warriors, hunters, and tribal members against vivid backgrounds and not in lonely rural scenes. One of his famous paintings shows a man in traditional costume, exhausted after a ritual dance, sitting with a pink ice cream cone in his hand. Scholder used his art to fight against the idea of Native American people as primitive or inferior, and challenged racist treatment of Native Americans in both laws and popular media.

Russell Means (1939-2012)

Russell Means, an Oglala Sioux, was an activist and film-maker. He helped found the American Indian Movement and pushed for more self-government for Native American tribes. He sometimes used violent methods, as when he took part in the takeover of the town of Wounded Knee, Minnesota, but was also active in more traditional politics. His efforts helped restore a sense of pride and dignity to many Native Americans.

Learn more about Native Americans

Wherever you are in North America, it was once land that Native Americans called their own. Who were the tribes that lived where you live now? You can honor them by learning more about them, perhaps from your local library.

52-05

Look further into Baby Professor books to learn more about peoples and cultures that have helped create the world you enjoy.

Visit

BABY PROFESSOR
EDUCATION KIDS

www.BabyProfessorBooks.com
to download Free Baby Professor eBooks
and view our catalog of new and exciting
Children's Books

www.ingramcontent.com/pod-product-compliance
Lightning Source LLC
Chambersburg PA
CBHW082000160726
47999CB00008B/2689